They Survived Mount St. Helens!

The amazing story of America's deadliest volcano

By Megan Stine

With photographs and illustrations

A Bullseye Nonfiction Book

Random House New York

Library of Congress Cataloging in Publication Data
Stine, Megan.
They survived Mount St. Helens / by Megan Stine.
  p. cm.—(A Bullseye nonfiction book)
"Read it to believe it"
Includes index.
SUMMARY: Describes the 1980 eruption of Mount St. Helens and the effects on those who experienced it firsthand.
ISBN: 0-679-84362-0 (pbk.)
1. Saint Helens, Mount (Wash.)—Eruption, 1980—Juvenile literature. [1. Saint Helens, Mount (Wash.)—Eruption, 1980. 2. Volcanoes.] I. Title.
QE 523.S23S75 1994 551.2'1'0979784—dc20 93-5505

Manufactured in the United States of America 10 9 8 7 6 5 4 3 2 1

Cover design by Michaelis/Carpelis Design Associates, Inc.

Photo credits: AP/Wide World Photos, 73, 79, 96–97; James Mason/Black Star, 30, 38–39; Ralph Perry/Black Star, 8, 47, 62–63, 88; James A. Sugar/Black Star, 82.

READ IT TO BELIEVE IT! is a trademark of Random House, Inc.

Contents

Chapter 1

"St. Helens Is Hot!"

"We want lava! We want lava!"

For weeks everyone in Washington had been waiting for Mount St. Helens to erupt. Some people were even *hoping* the volcano would explode.

They played songs about it on the radio. "We want lava!" were the words to one of the songs.

They wore T-shirts that said "I Lava Volcano" and "I Survived Mount St. Helens." Another T-shirt said "St. Helens Is Hot!"

The excitement had started on March 27, 1980. That's when Mount St. Helens—a volcanic mountain that had been asleep for 123 years—suddenly woke up. At a little past 12:30 in the afternoon, it shot a beautiful plume of ash and steam four miles into the sky.

The next day it erupted again. And then again.

All at once, the whole country got excited. A live volcano was erupting in the United States! This had never happened in modern times.

People from all over the world rushed to Washington State. Scientists were among the first to arrive. They couldn't wait to study the volcano and find out why it had come to life.

Geologists—scientists who learn about the history of the earth by studying rocks—had a theory. They said the eruption had been triggered by a series of small earthquakes under the mountain. Now the experts were watching to see what would happen next.

News reporters and photographers came too. They wrote stories about the volcano and took pictures of the plumes, which lingered for hours like beautiful fountains in the sky.

And local people were completely fascinated. Many of them wanted to see the smoke and ash for themselves. They drove to small towns near St. Helens' base. Then they sat in their cars, waiting for the eerie bursts of steam to shoot into the air. Everyone wanted to witness the giant mountain stirring to life.

Until this time Mount St. Helens had seemed like a quiet, beautiful, and safe place to be.

Spirit Lake, at the base of the mountain, was so clear that it reflected St. Helens like a mirror. Seen together, the lake and mountain looked like a picture postcard. Capping the mountain and adding to its peaceful beauty was a huge slab of ice and snow, called a glacier.

People lived and played on the mountain. Some went camping and fishing at Spirit Lake.

Before the blast: Spirit Lake at the base of Mount St. Helens. In a matter of days this area would look like the surface of the moon.

Others lived in nearby cabins and lodges. Boy scout and girl scout camps bustled with activity in spring and summer.

And hundreds of loggers worked on the

mountain, cutting down trees for the Weyer-haeuser logging company.

But now that the volcano had come to life, it wasn't so safe anymore.

Within a day of the first eruption, officials decided to close down the mountain. The loggers were sent home from their jobs. Then a 15-mile-wide area near the peak, labeled the red zone, was declared off-limits. Everyone who lived inside the red zone was ordered to leave.

No one could go near the top of the volcano without permission. The government set up roadblocks to keep people from driving in.

But one person refused to leave—83-year-old Harry Truman. Harry was a tough-minded old man who had lived on the mountain for more than fifty years. He owned a lodge in the red zone, near Spirit Lake.

Harry loved the mountain, and he just couldn't believe it might explode.

"I'm part of this mountain," Harry said. "It wouldn't dare blow up on me."

And besides, Harry claimed he had stock-piled enough food to last for 15 years! He wasn't worried about anything.

Soon Harry became famous. News reporters flocked to see him. They talked with him on the front porch of his lodge and wrote stories about him. They took pictures of him with his 16 cats. He became a hero because he wasn't afraid of the volcano.

Other people felt the same way. They thought, "That volcano will never explode." They wondered why they couldn't go back to work on the mountain. Or return to their cabins. Or go hiking and see the beautiful streams of smoke and ash.

Meanwhile, a small crater, or bowl-shaped opening in the earth, had developed near the mountain's top. Steam kept shooting into the air.

Sometimes the ash cloud was so high that it could be seen for miles around.

And there were earthquakes nearly every day.

But the eruptions were not large or fiery like some volcanoes. There was no hot flowing lava. No one got hurt.

Some people were disappointed. Others were bored. "We want lava!" they sang again and again.

But the lava didn't come.

And after a while, the mountain seemed to calm down. By April 30—five weeks after the first eruption—St. Helens had stopped puffing out steam. Nothing seemed to be happening.

Except that a bulge had formed on the mountain's north face.

The bulge was 300 feet high—as high as a 30-floor skyscraper—and almost a mile wide. And it was growing five feet higher every day!

Geologists worried about the lump. They knew it was a serious warning signal, telling them that hot melted rock was moving around underground. Soon the mountain could explode.

But most people didn't know about the bulge, so they didn't worry. They were used to the volcano by now.

So the government relaxed the rules. The loggers were allowed to go back to work.

Scientists were permitted on the mountain too. A team of geologists took turns watching the volcano. They set up seismometers—machines that measure the earth's shudders and shakes—all over St. Helens to help them monitor earthquakes and eruptions. Then they made camp on a ridge six miles from the peak. That seemed like a safe distance away.

And reporters were allowed to fly over. They weren't supposed to land anywhere near the volcano. But some of them broke the rules and set down near the top. One film crew even shot a beer commercial on the edge of the smoking crater.

Ordinary people sneaked into the red zone as well. Or they went near it, into the blue zone, which was farther away from the peak of the volcano. The blue zone wasn't off-limits, and it was supposed to be safe.

No one knew how dangerous the mountain really was, not even the scientists.

They had no idea that in a few weeks, 300 homes would be destroyed, more than 60 people would be dead, and every living thing in the path of the eruption would be wiped off the face of the earth.

Chapter 2

Fire Mountain

By early May 1980, it looked like St. Helens had gone back to sleep.

But she was still awake—and the geologists knew it.

How did they know? They did two things. They looked at a map, and they studied the history of the mountain itself.

Standing in the southwest corner of Washington State, St. Helens is part of a string of mountains called the Cascade Range.

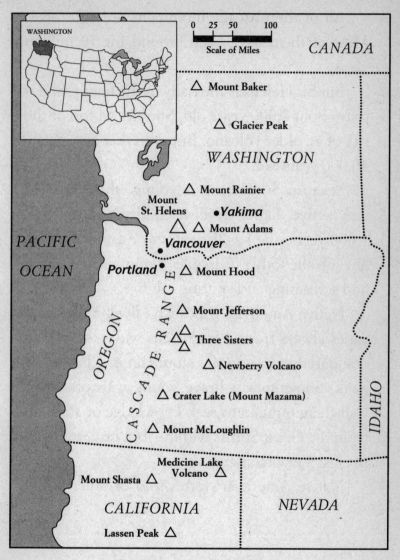

The Cascade mountain range.

All of the Cascade mountains are volcanoes. Most of them have been around for 50 million years.

But St. Helens is the baby in the family. She is only about 2,000 years old. She sits on top of the site of an older volcano. But even that one is only 40,000 years old.

Because St. Helens is young, she has been very active, like a devilish child. Over the past 1,000 years, she has thrown more tantrums than any of the other Cascade mountains—kicking and screaming and spitting out fire.

Native American tribes who lived in the Cascades always treated St. Helens with respect. No one dared to live on the mountain or climb to its peak. Sometimes a brave young warrior would visit the mountain to seek knowledge or strength from the Great Spirits within—but he would stay for just a few moments.

Native American stories told of other volcanoes, as well. In one story, Mount Adams and Mount Hood, the two mountains nearest to St. Helens, were said to be angry warriors. They battled over a beautiful young maiden, sending rocks and fire, thunder and smoke, into the sky.

When the battle was over, the young maiden was changed into a beautiful mountain—the mountain we call St. Helens.

The Native Americans had different names for her. Some tribes called her Loowit—Keeper of the Fire. The Klickitat Indians called her Tahonelatcah. In English, that means Fire Mountain.

In 1842, Fire Mountain started spitting out smoke and fumes and didn't stop completely until 1857.

Then she became dormant again. A dormant volcano is one that is not active, one that has gone to sleep.

The mountain slept for 100 years. Soon geologists began to wonder: when would the volcano erupt again?

In 1975, two scientists predicted that St. Helens would blow its top soon. Their names were Dwight "Rocky" Crandell and Donal Mullineaux. They said the mountain was due for a big eruption.

How did Crandell and Mullineaux know the mountain was going to erupt?

They dug around in the rocks near St. Helens and found ash that had come from the volcano long ago. They found plant material, too, and tested it to determine how old it was.

Some of the plants were about 100 years old. Some were 200 years old. Some were 300 years old, and so on.

The evidence pointed to one fact: Mount St. Helens was erupting like clockwork—about once every 100 years!

The last time had been in 1857. So by 1980, an eruption was *long* overdue.

The scientists also knew something else. They knew that Mount St. Helens was part of the Ring of Fire—a huge chain of volcanoes that circles the Pacific Ocean. Most of the volcanoes and earthquakes on earth are clustered around this one gigantic ring.

Why? To understand the answer, it helps to know how the earth is made.

The surface of the earth—the earth's crust—is made up of huge slabs, or plates. These plates float on hot melted rock, called magma, underneath. When magma comes out of the earth, it is called lava.

There is one big plate for each continent, and an especially huge plate under the Pacific Ocean. The Ring of Fire is the place where the continental plates meet the Pacific Ocean plate.

Sometimes the plates shift and bump into each other, causing earthquakes. Volcanoes erupt when the shifting plates allow magma to escape through a crack in the earth's crust.

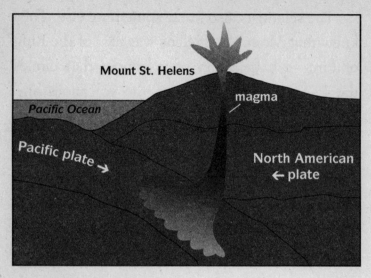

When one plate slides under another, magma is forced up to the surface.

That's what happened on March 20, 1980. One week before the first eruption of St. Helens, there was a small earthquake under the mountain. It measured 4.1 on the Richter scale—a numbering system that measures the strength of an earthquake.

The smallest quakes are less than 2.0 on the

scale and are not felt by human beings. The largest are 9.0 or more, resulting in total destruction.

The Ring of Fire—a circle of volcanoes around the Pacific Ocean.

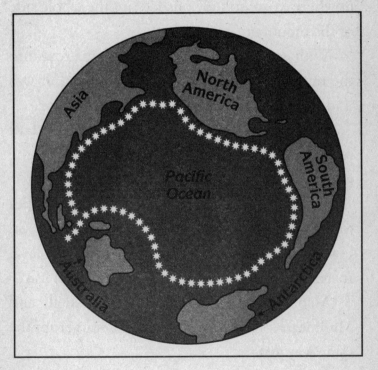

Other earthquakes followed.

And then the volcano began to erupt, and the bulge began to grow. The bulge was formed by magma rising up into the mountain. It was full of gases that were trying to expand. They had nowhere to go, so they pushed out the whole side of the mountain.

With each earthquake, more magma rose into the mountain. Like soda shaken in a can, it was under a lot of pressure—and ready to explode.

What would happen if it did? Would lava really pour out and run down the sides of the mountain?

The geologists didn't think so. Their studies told a different story. In the past, Mount St. Helens had almost never overflowed with lava. Instead, it usually sent up huge amounts of ash.

Many geologists—including Crandell and Mullineaux—thought St. Helens would erupt the same way again.

They thought that when the top of the mountain finally exploded, the magma would burn up into tiny pieces of ash.

That much turned out to be true.

But scientists thought they knew something else. They thought the ash would shoot out the top and straight up into the sky.

If they had known the truth—if they'd known how the mountain would *really* explode—they never would have allowed anyone near the top.

And they certainly wouldn't have been there themselves—only a few short miles away.

Chapter 3

"Vancouver!
This Is It!"

Saturday, May 17—the day before the mountain erupted—dawned crisp and clear. The sky sparkled brilliant blue. The air felt warm. And the snow-capped mountains shimmered in the distance.

Mike and Lu Moore decided to go camping.

The Moores lived in the Toutle River valley just 30 miles from the volcano. Lu had lived near the mountain since childhood. Now she and her husband had children of their own.

Bonnie Lu Moore was four years old. Terra, her baby sister, was only a few months old. It was going to be the girls' first camping trip.

The Moores packed their camping equipment with excitement. They loved the outdoors, and wanted to see if anything was happening on the mountain. Maybe it would erupt again! Maybe more smoke would come out!

Mike wanted to take more pictures. For weeks he had been photographing the changing mountain as the bulge grew bigger each day.

But Mike and Lu did not intend to get too close to the volcano—not close enough to be hurt. They certainly planned to stay out of the red zone. After all, they had two young children to protect.

Out of habit, Lu packed lots of water and enough dried food to last for two weeks. She always liked to be prepared. Mike packed all his camera equipment. They had a nice big tent. They were ready for anything.

At least that's what they thought.

The Moores were not the only people who went to the mountain that day. Hundreds of others were on or near St. Helens as well.

Some of them were fishing or camping or taking pictures, like the Moores. Others were loggers trying to earn extra money by working overtime.

And a small group of homeowners had returned to their cabins in the red zone, just for a few hours. They demanded to be allowed back in so they could remove some personal things— clothes, photo albums, jewelry, keepsakes—just in case the mountain blew.

And of course the scientists were there.

One was a young geologist named David Johnston. He was part of a team that worked for the USGS—the United States Geological Survey. The USGS offices were based in Vancouver, Washington, but the scientists took turns staying at the campsite on St. Helens itself. Their job was to watch the mountain and collect information about it.

Thirty-year-old Johnston knew the volcano was dangerous. A few weeks earlier he had even told reporters that being on the mountain was like "standing next to a dynamite keg with the fuse lit. Only we don't know how long that fuse is."

That weekend Johnston was not supposed to be on the mountain. It wasn't his turn. But another scientist had asked Johnston to take his place because he had something to do on Sunday morning.

So David Johnston had agreed. On Saturday afternoon he settled in at the campsite the scientists had named Coldwater II. The campsite consisted of some geological equipment and a trailer where Johnston would sleep that night. It was located on a ridge only six miles from the volcano.

That same afternoon, Mike and Lu Moore hiked up to a place called Gilbert Ridge. From there the Moores could see the volcano very well. They were not in the red zone, but they were quite close. If the mountain had blown then, they would have been killed.

But nothing was happening.

"We were bored," Lu said. "So we moved. We went to the Valley of the Giants."

The Valley of the Giants was named for the huge old trees that grew there. Some were so old they measured nine feet across. Lu and Mike found a beautiful spot near the Green River, about 13 miles north of the volcano.

They parked their car on the road, hiked up the trail about half a mile, and set up camp.

While they worked, Bonnie played and the baby stayed snug and happy in Lu's backpack.

Nearby was an old rundown cabin. The wood was rotting and the ceiling had holes.

Bonnie wanted to play in the cabin, but Lu said no, it wasn't safe.

That night everyone slept happily in the tent. The air was crisp and cold, the stars were bright.

Meanwhile, at Coldwater II, David Johnston got ready for bed. Before he went to sleep, he sent a radio message to the other scientists back in Vancouver. Everything was calm at the volcano, he told them. There was nothing new to report.

The next morning, Johnston woke up early. It was Sunday, May 18. Another bright, beautiful day.

Once again, Johnston radioed Vancouver to say there was no news.

But a short time later, at 8:32 A.M., something

happened. An earthquake rumbled under the volcano. It measured 5.0 on the Richter scale.

Moments later, the giant bulge on the side of the mountain simply slid away.

Johnston reached for his radio.

"Vancouver! Vancouver! This is it!" he shouted.

Those were the last words he ever spoke.

In the next instant, the volcano exploded with the force of 10 to 50 megaton bombs—500 times more powerful than the bomb that destroyed Hiroshima, Japan, during World War II.

But to everyone's amazement, the volcano did not explode straight up. Not at first. Instead it blew sideways, blasting out the entire north side of the mountain.

In an instant, 400 million tons of rock were turned into dust and hurled into the air. Boulders the size of trucks flew out with the force of a hurricane wind. A sea of hot poisonous gases and molten rock—called a pyroclastic flow—poured down the mountain like liquid at 100 miles an hour.

And Coldwater II, where David Johnston was stationed, lay right in the path of the blast.

A few miles away, at the USGS campsite called Coldwater I, was photographer Reid Blackburn. He worked for a newspaper in Vancouver, but he had been hired by the USGS to take pictures of the volcano.

Reid saw the explosion as it happened. Quickly he clicked off a few pictures, then ran to his car.

He, too, was in the direct path of the eruption, only eight miles from the top.

Thirteen miles from the mountain, the Moores were making breakfast when they heard an odd sound and looked up. They could not see the mountain from where they were, because their campsite was down in a valley.

But an enormous dark cloud filled the sky as

they watched, bigger and blacker than anything they'd ever seen.

They knew immediately what it meant. The volcano had erupted—and a cloud of dense dark ash was coming their way!

As quickly and calmly as she could, Lu began to pack up the camping gear so she could move Bonnie and Terra to safety.

She didn't rush. That was something Lu had learned from her father when she was a little girl: Never hurry in an emergency. Because when you hurry, Lu's father had always said, mistakes can happen.

So Lu stayed calm—but she had to think fast. Where could she move her children?

She knew the answer right away. The old broken-down cabin!

Yesterday she had thought the cabin was dangerous. But now that the mountain was erupting, it was the safest place to be!

The cloud moved quickly, blocking out the

sun. In those few minutes before total darkness, Mike took some pictures. Then he ran to join his family in the cabin.

Soon it was completely dark—blacker than midnight—at 8:30 in the morning! Mike and Lu couldn't see a thing.

They huddled in the pitch-dark cabin with their children, wondering what would happen next.

Ash fell like snow outside. It sifted through the holes in the cabin's roof. Lu and Mike knew they might die if they breathed it in.

They put the baby on a table and covered her with a blanket to keep the dust off her face and out of her lungs. Then Lu found some of Bonnie's socks. She wet them and gave one to her daughter.

"Put the sock over your mouth," she told Bonnie. "And breathe through it."

Lu and Mike did the same thing. They knew that would keep out the dust.

But even with the socks, it was hard not to breathe the ash. A thick layer of it settled on everything. It rose up and filled the air whenever anyone moved.

For a long, long time, the Moores sat in the dark and waited. Waited and wondered how long the darkness would last—and whether or not they would survive.

Chapter 4

Terror in the Blue Zone

Not far from Lu and Mike Moore, six young friends from the Mount St. Helens area were camping. They had picked a spot along the Green River that seemed perfectly safe. It was in the blue zone, about 12 miles from the top of the volcano. They couldn't even see the mountain from where they were.

Bruce Nelson had awakened early that Sunday morning. So had his 21-year-old girlfriend,

Sue Ruff. They got busy making coffee while their friend Terry Crall went fishing in the Green River. Terry's girlfriend, Karen Varner, was still sleeping in their tent.

Two other friends, Brian and Dan, were just waking up. They were camped nearby.

Suddenly Terry came running back to camp. He had hooked a fish, but he needed a new fishing line to reel it in. He was excited.

Just then he looked up at the sky and saw a strange cloud.

"Hey, Bruce," Terry said. "I think there's a forest fire."

Bruce looked up and shook his head. "That's no forest fire," he said.

And then, all at once, everyone knew. The mountain had blown up!

Sue ran to Bruce and threw her arms around him. She held on tight. They didn't know what to do. There was nowhere to run, no place to hide.

They stood for a moment and watched the

ash cloud form—a huge mushrooming mountain of smoke that seemed to rise for miles into the sky.

Bruce thought it was beautiful and breathtak-
ing. But within minutes it had engulfed the sky.
Terry Crall ran to wake up his girlfriend.

"Karen!" he called as he dived into their tent.

That was the last thing Bruce heard from his friend.

A moment later, the sky went black and banging sounds filled the air. Bruce and Sue stood there in shock, terrified and confused by all the noise.

Suddenly they tumbled and fell.

And then, a moment later, it became quiet— so quiet they couldn't understand how it could be that way.

The sky was still pitch-black. In the dark, Bruce couldn't see his own hand in front of his face. He tasted dirt in his mouth.

"Are you okay?" he asked Sue.

"Yes," she said. Her voice sounded muffled, as if they were buried underground.

Bruce thought they had fallen into a hole. Or maybe the hill nearby had crashed down and buried them.

He started to climb out, but when he reached the top of the hole, he was suddenly knocked back—by a tremendous wave of heat! It washed over him, burning the hair off his arms.

"We're dead! We're dead!" Bruce moaned as he fell back into the hole.

"We're not dead yet," Sue said. "Keep digging."

Bruce climbed up again, crawling over timber that had fallen all around. Luckily, the heat wave was gone; it hadn't lasted very long. He helped Sue out of the hole, but it was still too dark to see. And now the quiet had ended.

Thunder and lightning crashed and sparked above their heads. They looked up and saw the ash cloud all around them—and it was filled with its own thunderstorms!

"Everything came in stages," Bruce said later. "The blast. The heat. The quiet. The noise."

Now a new stage began—the falling ash.

The ash was so hot it burned their eyes. It choked their throats and made them feel as if they couldn't breathe.

Quickly Bruce and Sue yanked off their sweatshirts and wrapped them around their faces to keep the ash out of their lungs.

We've got to get to higher ground to find air, Bruce thought.

So they stumbled around in the dark, climbing over logs, trying to move away from the rainstorm of ash.

But it wasn't raining only ash. Pieces of wood, rock, and ice from the glacier were falling from the sky too.

And then, for just a few moments, the huge cloud moved. Light came through, and Bruce and Sue could see.

And what they saw was horrible.

Trees were down everywhere, in every direction—many that had been standing for centuries.

Some had been pulled up by the roots. Others had simply snapped off.

Nothing had any color in it. Everything that had been green before—the grass, the flowers, the shrubs and trees—was either burned black or covered with fine gray ash.

It was an absolute nightmare. It looked like a nuclear bomb had been dropped—or like they had landed on the moon.

Then Bruce saw the hole they had climbed out of. It had been made when two huge trees were uprooted. Bruce and Sue had fallen into the space where the roots used to be.

Quickly, Sue took out her contact lenses so she could rub the ash out of her eyes.

Bruce began calling for their friends. "Terry! Karen!" he yelled.

No one answered.

Then the sky grew dark again. Bang! Something crashed down in the distance.

The nightmare hadn't ended!

Earthquakes rippled the ground, knocking Bruce and Sue off the logs they were straddling.

If they were going to survive, they had to find someplace safe!

Feeling his way in the dark, Bruce found a huge tree that lay across a tangle of other trees. He and Sue crawled under it. Maybe they would be safe there—safe from the trees that were still crashing down around them. Safe from the lightning bolts that kept slicing down from the sky.

In the dark, under the tree, Bruce and Sue talked about a lot of things. About their fears. And about the future.

"If we get out of here alive," Bruce said, "I want to marry you."

But Bruce didn't think they *would* get out alive.

Chapter 5

The Whole World Watches

For the next hour or so, Bruce and Sue huddled in the darkness, protected by the tree. A few miles away, the Moore family crouched in the pitch-black cabin.

None of them had any idea how large the eruption had been.

They didn't know that the first sideways blast produced a landslide which ripped out the side of the mountain—not in one big bang, but with an explosion that lasted nearly 15 minutes. Or that St. Helens then erupted upward—and would spit ash into the sky for the next nine hours straight.

But outside the blast zone, thousands of people knew that something terrible had happened. They saw the ash cloud growing to a frightening size. Within 15 minutes, it reached 10 miles into the air!

As the wind blew, the cloud spread out and moved east. Within an hour, it had reached Yakima, Washington, the nearest big city. By 9:30 in the morning, the sky was as dark as night and the streetlights came on by themselves. In an area 200 miles wide, car headlights could not pierce the darkness.

People began coughing and choking in the streets. Car engines stalled and died because the ash clogged the air filters.

By day's end the ash cloud had reached Wyoming.
In 17 days it would circle the earth.

By the end of the day, the ash had drifted as far east as Wyoming, a thousand miles away, writing a dark message of doom across the sky.

People who did not see the cloud heard the eruption. It came as a terrible booming sound that shook the earth. The noise was heard as far away as Saskatchewan, Canada—690 miles north of the mountain's peak.

Oddly, though, most of the people on or near the mountain did not hear a thing. A strange "circle of silence" had surrounded the eruption, and people who lived within 60 miles of the mountain did not hear it blow up. Later, scientists explained the silence, saying that sound waves traveled differently in the heated air.

Jim and Nancy Althof were among the people who heard nothing. They lived beside the Toutle River in Castle Rock, Washington, about 30 miles from the volcano.

At 9:30 that morning, the sheriff knocked on Jim and Nancy's door. He had come to tell them to leave their house because the mountain had erupted.

"We don't know what's going to happen next," the sheriff said, sounding worried.

But they all knew what *might* happen.

For weeks everyone had been talking about how an eruption could affect the Toutle River.

If lava flowed out of the volcano, it would probably follow the natural valleys. The Toutle River also followed the valleys. People feared that lava would flow into the Toutle and fill it up, causing a flood.

But what happened was much worse.

Instead of lava, there was an enormous explosion of hot rock, gas, and ash. It sent the bulge hurtling down the mountain, creating a deadly and terrifying landslide.

Then, as gases from the blast reached a temperature of 900° Fahrenheit, the glacier melted, producing 46 billion gallons of water. That's as much water as there is in the Great Salt Lake!

All that water mixed with the ash, rocks, and

thousands of fallen trees to form a mudslide so powerful, it could knock bridges right off their foundations.

As the sheriff stood on the Althofs' doorstep, a wall of mud was already oozing downhill, like an ocean of wet cement.

The mudflow moved slowly at first, but eventually it would reach a top speed of 50 miles per hour.

And it gathered up everything in its path. Dead animals, cars, logs, even people—all were swept along as the mudflow grew bigger and bigger.

No one knew when or where it would stop.

But Jim and Nancy Althof weren't too worried. Their house was above the level of the river, 25 feet back from the bank. And they lived 30 miles from the volcano. How could the mudflow come so far? Wouldn't it slow down and stop before it reached their house?

Just the same, the sheriff had ordered them to leave. So Nancy packed up her photo albums. If anything in the house got wet, she didn't want her family photos to be ruined.

Jim moved their cars and their camp trailer to higher ground. Then he and Nancy went to a little store about a quarter of a mile away.

Other families were gathering in the store too. Everyone was glued to the radio there, eager for news of the eruption. But the reports came in slowly, and no one had any details.

Still, Jim and Nancy felt sure their house and possessions were safe. But they hadn't seen the mudflow yet, and they didn't know how fast it was moving.

They hadn't seen the ash cloud either.

In fact, no one in the little town of Castle Rock had seen it, because the huge cloud was drifting eastward, and Castle Rock was to the west.

That's why all the families to the west of the mountain sat calmly by—completely unaware that debris from the biggest landslide in recorded history was headed their way.

Chapter 6

Darkness and Destruction

Crash! Boom!

The mountain kept on rumbling.

Huddled under the tree in the dark, it was hard for Bruce and Sue to know what the sounds meant.

The trees had already fallen, so what was all that crashing? Was something *else* going to tumble down on them?

Was the darkness ever going to pass?

Before the blast, Bruce had not been a very religious person. But now, as he sat under the log, he prayed.

Finally the ash-filled sky began to get light. Bruce and Sue stood up and headed back to their campsite.

Was anyone else alive?

It was strangely quiet, Bruce thought. Too quiet. There were no birds singing.

And where was the camp? It was hard to tell because everything looked different. Everything was gray.

Everything except Sue and Bruce. Their skin was red, as if they'd been out in the sun too long. The heat wave had given them a light burn.

The ash below their feet was still hot too—so hot that it almost melted their boots.

Suddenly Bruce heard someone cry out. It was Dan!

Bruce and Sue ran to help him. But there wasn't much they could do.

Dan was nearly in shock. The skin had been burned off his arms. His fingers had swollen to the size of sausages. His feet were burned, too, because he wasn't wearing shoes.

Dan's friend Brian was nearby, under a tree. The tree had fallen on him and crushed his hip.

Bruce had to do something—but what? He looked around and saw an old miner's cabin nearby. Using wood from the cabin, he and Sue made a shelter to protect Brian from the falling ash. Bruce also gave Brian his shirt. Then he and Sue got ready to go.

"Don't leave me here to die!" Brian pleaded.

Bruce tried not to listen. He knew that none of them would survive unless he went for help.

Dan could hardly walk, but he hiked with Bruce and Sue to the Green River. Without shoes, the ash burned his feet with every step.

Finally Bruce decided he had to leave Dan behind too. Dan could soak his burned arms and legs in the river. Bruce and Sue would go on and get help.

They walked for hours. Mile after mile, the things they saw were terrible. Herds of elk wandered around, dazed. The elk had been hit by the blast. On one side—the side facing the blast—the animals were badly burned. The other side was unharmed.

The elk were confused. They let Bruce and Sue come right up to them.

Then, in the silence, Bruce saw birds. They were alive, but they couldn't fly. They fluttered helplessly on the ground.

And not once did Bruce and Sue hear an airplane.

Bruce began to wonder. How big had the blast been? Was anyone looking for them? Maybe all the towns around the base of the mountain had been destroyed!

By now Bruce and Sue were in a lot of pain. Their eyes burned from the ash. But they couldn't wash them out. They couldn't drink, either, because the water in the Green River was no longer safe. It smelled like rotten eggs—the smell of the chemical sulfur. Bruce knew that sulfur was poisonous. And besides, the river was filled with ash.

Finally, near dark, they made their way out of the blast zone. They had hiked almost 18 miles. But they were still in the wilderness—still a long way from home.

As they walked along a logging road, they suddenly saw another person—an older man. His name was Grant Christensen. Grant was a logger who had tried to drive up to the mountain after the blast. He wanted to get some tools that he had left in a logging camp up there.

But the heat and ash had ruined Grant's truck. Now he was lost too.

With Grant's help, Bruce and Sue found a

spring. Fresh water! It felt so good to wash out their eyes and take a drink.

Then the three survivors walked on together. Bruce and Sue were experienced hikers and knew the landscape, so they headed north, away from the volcano and toward the public roads. Finally they came to a logging road, but no one was there. No rescuers. No signs of life.

It was almost dark, about 7:30 at night, and starting to get cold. Even in May, temperatures could drop to 40 degrees at night on the mountain. Bruce thought they'd better find some firewood, so he went into the woods with Sue and Grant.

Suddenly they heard the whir of a helicopter. At last! They were going to be saved!

But the pilot couldn't see them because they were hidden by trees. They ran out of the woods and onto the road just as the pilot turned to leave.

Quickly Bruce and Sue beat the ash-covered ground with their sweatshirts. The ash rose up into the air, making a huge dust cloud.

Did the pilot see it?

Yes!

Slowly he turned the helicopter around and landed in the only clear place he could find, about a mile away.

Bruce and Sue raced toward the helicopter. Mike Cairns, the pilot, jumped out and ran toward Sue.

"We're so glad to find you!" Mike cried. His voice cracked as he threw his arms around her.

Cairns was filled with emotion. Later, Bruce found out why.

All day the rescuers had been finding nothing but dead bodies on the mountain. Mike Cairns had seen a truck with three people sitting in it— all dead.

Sue and Bruce were the first people he had found alive!

Now that they were safe, Bruce knew they had to hurry. There were still other survivors to be rescued.

Quickly, Bruce, Sue, and Grant climbed into the helicopter. Then Bruce told Mike Cairns where to go. Dan and Brian were badly hurt. They needed help fast. And what about Terry and Karen?

Cairns flew toward the campsite on the river. "How far is it?" he yelled to Bruce over the roar of the chopper.

"Keep going!" Bruce said.

Cairns wasn't sure. Maybe Bruce was wrong.

"There's no way anyone could be alive this far up the mountain," Cairns said.

Besides, Cairns had orders not to fly too far into the blast zone. The ash might ruin the helicopter's motor.

"Keep going!" Bruce insisted. He peered down at the river. Everything looked so different. The only things Bruce recognized were the bridges across the Green River. He knew he had parked his truck by a bridge, so he counted them to keep track of how far they had come.

"Keep going!"

Finally Bruce spotted the bridge he was looking for and saw his truck, covered with ash.

Mike Cairns looked for a place to land, but there was no room. He radioed for a smaller helicopter to help them out.

Soon the smaller chopper arrived and landed on the bridge. But there was no one in sight. Where were Dan and Brian?

The pilot got out and started to wade through the ash along the bridge. Suddenly a human head popped up out of the dust.

It was Brian! He was still alive! Even with a crushed hip, he had dragged himself all the way

*Rescue workers
found two victims in
this truck, suffocated
by ash.*

from the shelter to the bridge. When the helicopter landed, it had buried him in ash.

After strapping Brian to one of the helicopter

runners, the small chopper returned to the air-port. Mike Cairns and Bruce searched for Dan, Terry, and Karen a while longer, but found no one. Finally, under orders, the pilot returned to base.

Later, Bruce found out that Dan had been picked up by another rescue team.

Now there was only one question still gnawing at Bruce's heart.

Where were Terry and Karen—and could they still be alive?

Chapter 7

Mud and Tears

All that Sunday afternoon, the rescue helicopters flew over the mountain. But none of them came near the old cabin where the Moore family had been huddled in the dark that morning, waiting for the ash to stop.

Lu Moore tried to stay calm. But it was so dark in the cabin, she couldn't even see her children. The baby lay perfectly quiet under the blanket on the table.

Was she okay?

Mike Moore reached out and shook the baby's leg. Terra let out a little squawk.

At least now they knew she was still alive!

Finally, as the ash cloud moved, the cabin began to get light. The sun didn't shine brightly, as it had before the eruption. But the sky wasn't as dark as midnight now.

Lu and Mike gathered up their things. They put the baby in Lu's backpack and collected their other gear.

Then they started back down the trail. But where was it? Lu and Mike couldn't tell, because dull gray ash covered everything.

In fact, the whole world was gray and brown, like the surface of the moon.

Still, the Moores thought they could find their way back to their car. After all, they had parked only half a mile away.

They walked down the trail for a few minutes and then stopped.

Wait a minute, Lu thought. Why were there so many fallen trees on the trail? She and Mike felt confused.

They didn't know that thousands of trees had been knocked down during the blast. Their campsite was in a protected spot, behind a ridge. Many of the trees nearby were still standing.

But the trees that had fallen on the trail made it look so different that Lu and Mike didn't recognize it. Maybe this wasn't the trail at all, they thought. Maybe they were lost.

They turned around, went back a short way, and started over, trying to find the trail again.

For five hours Lu and Mike searched for the trail—even though they were on it all the time!

Finally they came to a place that had not been protected from the blast. Hundreds of trees were blown down flat.

"It looked like someone had taken an eggbeater and stirred up all the trees," Lu said.

Tree trunks lay everywhere, like giant toothpicks. Every inch of bark, every leaf, had been burned off.

Now Mike and Lu began to be afraid. Now they understood how enormous the blast had been. And maybe the volcano would erupt again! Maybe more trees would fall and kill them.

A terrible rumbling sound had been following them all day, too, like a huge cement mixer.

The Moores didn't know that it was the sound of more trees falling, and the mudflow picking up rocks and ice as it swept down the mountainside. All they knew was that the sound tore at their nerves, making them more afraid.

Bonnie tried to be brave. She seemed to understand that this was an emergency. Even though she was only four years old, she didn't whine or complain. But Lu could tell she was getting tired.

By late afternoon, Lu and Bonnie were exhausted. They had spent hours hiking with their heavy packs, climbing over fallen trees. The deadly ash lay everywhere.

Tears began to run down Bonnie's cheeks. Mike took out his camera and snapped a few pictures of her. That usually cheered her up.

But slowly, Mike and Lu realized the truth. They were not going to reach their car today. They were going to have to spend the night on the mountain.

They had used the last of their water hours ago, and the dust was making them all very thirsty.

They were hungry, too, but they couldn't eat. All they had was dried food. It had to be mixed with water before it could be used.

Mike looked around. There must be something he could do. He was not going to give up!

Just then he saw a stream. It was covered with

branches and mud, but he could see fresh water underneath. He scooped the mud and pulled the branches away.

At last! Water to drink!

Now all they had to do was set up their tent—and try to sleep through the long night.

But Lu had a hard time getting any rest. There were too many things to worry about.

Would the mountain erupt again?

When would they be rescued?

And what was that smell?

All at once, Lu knew. Forest fires! It smelled as if trees were burning all over the mountain.

Lying under the stars on the desolate mountain, Lu worried about the fires—and about whether they would spread to her family's campsite that night.

Meanwhile, in the town of Castle Rock, the mudflow oozed closer.

Jim and Nancy Althof heard about it late that afternoon, from some people who dashed into the little store.

"It's coming down the Toutle River," someone said.

That's what everyone had expected. But no one knew how big the mudflow was.

Jim Althof began to feel restless. He wanted information and he wasn't getting it. So he decided to go back home. At least there he could watch the news on TV! Maybe then he would find out what was going on.

Jim went back to his house by the river and sat watching TV. Suddenly he heard a strange noise. He ran outside and looked at the river. The mudflow was surging down the Toutle— headed right toward him!

Heart pounding, Jim knew he had to get out of there fast.

Quickly he raced back to the store to get

Nancy. Then they drove to a friend's house. The friend lived high on a bluff overlooking the river. Up there, Jim and Nancy knew they would be safe.

Too bad they couldn't move their house to higher ground as well.

Because all of a sudden Nancy smelled something awful—like rotten eggs mixed with wet cement.

And then they saw it. The mudflow—worse than they ever imagined. It was higher than the house. Higher than everything except the tallest trees.

Nancy and Jim stood on the cliff, watching in horror as the mudflow hit their house and knocked it off its foundation. Within minutes the house was completely swept away.

Then they watched as their neighbors' houses were destroyed as well.

"Cars and trucks floated by like toys," Nancy said.

A farmer slogs through the aftermath with inner tubes strapped to his feet. All of his grazing land was buried by mud.

Other houses, from farther up the river, drifted by too.

The next day, Nancy and Jim walked along the river and found that what they feared was true. Their house had been broken into so many pieces that there was nothing left of it.

But as they walked farther, Nancy saw something white in the mud. Their freezer! The food in it was still good!

A while later, she found her refrigerator with a glass bowl inside—and the bowl wasn't even cracked.

For the next few days, Nancy and her husband kept looking along the river. It was like a treasure hunt. They wondered what they would discover next.

To their surprise, they found a chest of drawers. The fronts of all the drawers had been torn off. Jim's clothes were inside, soaked with mud. But Nancy washed them, and Jim wore them after that.

Another time, they found their copper teapot. The lid was still on, but the teapot was filled with mud.

"The more we looked, the funnier it got," Nancy said.

But the best was saved for last. One day a neighbor girl came up to Nancy, carrying a small plastic box.

"Is this yours?" the girl asked.

Nancy looked at it. Her heart leaped.

Yes! It was Nancy's. Inside were two of her dearest treasures. One was a watch that Nancy's mother had given to her for her eighth-grade graduation.

The other was a pin—a double heart with her parents' names on it. Nancy's and her brother's names were engraved on it too.

Nancy couldn't believe it. The plastic box wasn't even dirty!

It was amazing to Nancy—but true. Enough mud had come down the Toutle River to raise the water level by 66 feet. There was so much mud that in places it rolled over hills 300 feet high. Eight large bridges had been knocked off their foundations by the flow.

But somehow—even with all of that destruction—a few precious keepsakes had been saved. Nancy was glad to have them, and even more grateful to be alive.

Chapter 8

The Morning After

The day after the eruption was a disaster for nearly everyone.

Ash lay everywhere. It covered lawns and gardens, sidewalks and streets. Every car, every house, every leaf, every tree, was gray with ash.

When people stepped outside, their feet kicked up the ash and made dust clouds.

It was five inches deep in some places. In other places, it was still falling!

So many car air filters became clogged that

more than half the police cars and emergency vehicles in the state of Washington were unable to move.

Even airplanes were affected by the ash. Planes were grounded for days. No one could go anywhere. More than 3,000 people were stranded away from home.

Some people rushed out and bought extra air filters—or made them out of pantyhose so they could drive their cars. But then they ran into another problem. Driving down the ash-filled streets stirred up small white dust clouds, making it impossible to see. People crashed into telephone poles and hit other drivers.

There were 600,000 tons of ash on the streets and lawns and houses of Yakima alone. Across the state of Washington was enough ash to fill your house a million times!

People began to worry. Was it safe to breathe the ash?

Many experts said no. They told the public to

One week after the eruption, ash still
clogged the air for miles around.

wear dust masks over their mouths when they went outdoors.

But there weren't enough masks in the entire state for all the people who needed them.

The 3M company sent one million masks to Washington. Even that wasn't enough. Some families had to breathe through wet wash-cloths—or go without.

People tried to shovel the ash away. But where could they put it? There was enough ash in Yakima alone to fill 100,000 dump trucks. But the trucks weren't running!

Monday was disastrous for other reasons, too. Hundreds of people waited anxiously for news of family members who had been near the moun-tain when it blew.

Rescue teams and helicopters had pulled out nearly 190 people in the hours after the blast. But dozens more were still missing.

Could any of them still be alive?

One family was doing fine. On Monday morning the Moores woke up early, happy to be safe. The forest fires hadn't come near them.

They made breakfast, then hiked back to the clearing they had seen the day before.

The Moores knew they had to stay out in the open if a rescue helicopter was going to find them. And they knew that rescue teams were flying in the area, because they had heard a chopper the night before.

Now all they had to do was wait.

It wasn't long before an Air Force helicopter appeared, hovering overhead. But did the pilot see them?

Yes!

The only problem was that the pilot couldn't land. Every time he brought the chopper down, the blades stirred up so much dust that no one could see. It was like being caught in a "white-out." That's what skiers call it when a snowstorm is so blinding that all you can see is white.

The Moores watched as the helicopter rose

*Superhot air and hurricane-force winds destroyed
every tree in a 200-square-mile area.*

into the air again. Then the door opened and two shapes fell from the sky.

Parajumpers!

When they landed, they told Mike and Lu not to worry. Soon a smaller helicopter would arrive.

When it came, it hovered low over the Green River where there was less ash.

Lu, Mike, and Bonnie walked out to it. The river was shallow, and they made their way on the rocks and sand.

But when they tried to climb inside the helicopter, the pilot shook his head. The space was very small.

"You can't bring your backpacks!" he yelled. "There's no room!"

The helicopter motor was so loud that Lu couldn't hear him. She tried to climb into the helicopter again.

The pilot grabbed her backpack and tried to

throw it in the river. He thought it was full of food and clothes and other things that could be replaced.

Lu held on tight. The backpack had her baby in it! Little Terra Moore was zipped up inside!

The pilot pulled hard on the pack. Lu pulled harder. She tried to explain, but it was no use. The pilot couldn't hear a word she said.

Finally the pilot gave up. He thought Lu was crazy. He thought she wouldn't give up her food and clothes. There was no point in fighting with her.

When the struggle was over, the helicopter lifted off. Then the pilot could hear. Mike told him their baby was in the pack.

A baby? Amazing!

The pilot was glad he hadn't dumped her in the river after all!

Chapter 9

Is Anyone Else Alive?

By Thursday, the fourth day after the blast, Bruce Nelson was going crazy.

News reporters had been hounding him day and night. Everyone wanted to hear his story. After all, he was one of the few people who had survived the mountain's terrifying blast.

But something else was hounding Bruce as well.

Thoughts of Terry and Karen.

Bruce couldn't help wondering: could they possibly still be alive?

For four days, the families of the missing young people had been asking Bruce questions.

Where were Terry and Karen when the mountain blew? Why didn't Bruce see them when he stumbled into Brian and Dan? And most importantly: Could Bruce find the campsite if he went back in?

Bruce knew the answer to the last question.

Yes—he felt sure he could locate the campsite again. In fact, he thought he was the *only* person who could.

And he wanted desperately to go.

But no one would take him. Civilians were still not allowed into the blast zone.

The area was off-limits for a lot of reasons. For one, the mountain was still erupting! Every once in a while, more smoke shot up from the huge crater left by the blast.

For another, rescuers were still looking for dead bodies. It would be weeks before all the victims were found.

And scientists did not want people tramping around in the blast zone. The whole mountain was like a huge outdoor laboratory to them—a once-in-a-lifetime chance to study the effects of an eruption right after it happened. If civilians were allowed in, they might destroy important scientific information.

In the meantime, rescuers continued to hope for survivors. But all they saw were more signs of death.

Reid Blackburn's body was eventually found at the Coldwater I campsite. The photographer had taken a few final pictures just as the mountain erupted. Then he fled to his car.

When he was finally found, he was wrapped in a blanket in the car, buried in ash.

Other bodies were found in strange places. Four loggers who had been working on the

*Reid Blackburn was found in his car—barely
visible in the middle of this photo.*

mountain that Sunday were badly burned. Three of them managed to walk to safety and were taken to the hospital. But only one of them lived.

The fourth man's body was found in a tree. He had climbed up there to escape the burning ash, and had died before he could come down.

Harry Truman, the man who refused to leave the mountain, had died on it. His lodge at Spirit Lake was buried under the landslide of rock, mud, and ash.

Perhaps most horrifying was the fate of David Johnston, the young geologist at Coldwater II. His campsite was only six miles away from the volcano—too close for any chance of survival.

When the blast hit, he was blown off the ridge along with his Jeep and his trailer in a heat wave that vaporized everything.

His body was never found.

But what about Terry and Karen?

Bruce knew that their parents couldn't wait much longer.

Finally, on Thursday, Bruce got a break. That morning he was asked to appear on television, on the *Today* show.

After the interview, one of the *Today* reporters offered to help Bruce go find his friends.

Great! Bruce thought.

They went to the airport, and the reporter hired a helicopter. But then they ran into the same old problem—officials at the airport wouldn't let them take off.

The rules were still in force. No civilians allowed.

For a while Bruce waited and argued, trying to explain who he was and what he wanted to do.

People were already wearing T-shirts that said "I Survived Mount St. Helens." But for Bruce, it was really true!

And now he was trying to find two more survivors. But no one would listen to him.

Finally the reporter got mad. He turned on his camera and pointed it at the people who were in charge.

"You take Bruce up there to go find his friends—right now!" the reporter said. Or else!

Everyone knew what the reporter meant. He would make the officials at the airport look bad, right then and there, on national TV.

Within minutes Bruce was in the air, flying in a helicopter with the pilot and two other rescue workers.

They landed near the campsite and hiked into the woods, but at first Bruce couldn't find the tent. Then finally he saw it.

A tree was lying across the tent.

And Terry and Karen were inside.

They had died instantly when the tree fell on them. Terry's arm was draped over Karen, as if he had been trying to protect her.

It was a horrible day for Bruce. Much worse

than the day the mountain blew up. Finding his friends that way was terrible.

But the experience wasn't over yet.

Suddenly Bruce saw that there were more survivors! Four who had lived through the blast and were still alive, even though it was days later!

Four more people to rescue?

No. These survivors were small and fuzzy. They were dogs!

It was almost too good to be true.

Terry Crall had brought a dog and her pups along with him on the camping trip. Wonderful German shepherds. Now the mama was pinned under a tree. But she was still alive!

Her tail wagged slightly when she saw Bruce. Her three puppies were huddled around her. They had stayed close to their mama for four whole days.

Bruce grabbed a chainsaw and went to work, first cutting one side of the tree, then another.

Finally, he lifted the tree away from the mother dog.

He held her in his arms, wondering if she was injured. Would she survive?

She hadn't eaten in four days. She hadn't had any water, except maybe a few licks of rainwater.

But she was a strong dog. And maybe she knew her puppies needed her!

After a while Bruce put her down. And she was able to walk to the helicopter all by herself.

Bruce carried the three puppies in his back-pack. "They looked like little ash balls," he said.

When he got home, Bruce took the dogs to Terry's parents. They let Bruce keep one of the puppies. It lived to be 12 years old. But the mother dog lived longer, and is still alive today.

She and her puppies were the last survivors ever found on the mountain.

Chapter 10

Forever Changed

When Mount St. Helens erupted, it left its footprints of destruction on nearly everything in its path and changed everything in its shadow forever.

It changed the landscape. The mountain had been almost 9,700 feet tall. Now it was less than 8,400 feet tall.

A whole side of the mountain had been blasted away, leaving a huge crater at the top instead of a peak. The crater was a mile wide and almost a mile deep.

The blast changed the lakes and rivers. The Toutle River had been an unspoiled fisherman's paradise, winding past cabins and houses in small towns north and west of the mountain. Now it was paved with gooey, stinking mud.

Spirit Lake—once beautiful and crystal clear—was now a sea of mud filled with dead fish, sulfur, rocks, logs, and ash.

The blast changed the wildlife. More than a million birds and animals died. Eagles, owls, cougars, black bears, mountain goats, huge herds of deer and elk—all were either killed instantly by the blast or, miles away, choked to death by ash.

Eleven million fish died—some suffocated by ash, others nearly boiled alive. The mudflows raised the temperature of the water to almost 100° Fahrenheit—so hot that salmon jumped out of the rivers, trying to escape!

The forests changed too. Every single tree within eight miles of the mountaintop was

stripped of its leaves and bark and knocked flat. More than 60,000 acres of forest were ruined— enough timber to build 80,000 houses. The

Harry Truman and his lodge are buried somewhere beneath Spirit Lake, shown here at the base of a dormant (for now) St. Helens.

owls and eagles that survived the blast had nowhere to live.

And all the towns around the mountain

changed. Many people could not stand to live near the volcano anymore. They packed up and moved to other states.

Some people left because the ash just wouldn't go away.

"You wash it off your porches, sidewalks, and streets in the morning," one person said, "and by the afternoon it's back."

Crops in Washington were ruined by the ash. Under the weight of it, whole fields of alfalfa were smashed flat.

But farmers tried to look on the bright side. Even though they were losing crops now, they knew that the ash would be good for the soil in the future. It would make the soil richer so that harvests would be bountiful in coming years.

The only people who really liked the ash were the people who sold it. Gift shop owners in California came to Washington and scooped up the ash. They took it home, put it in packets, and sold the packets for several dollars each.

Of course, no one in Washington wanted to buy ash! But many people kept some as a souvenir. They still have it today.

Washington residents also tried to mail the ash to friends around the country. Then another problem popped up. Envelopes full of ash broke open in the post office and clogged the postal machines.

Worst of all, the ash had been a killer of human beings. When doctors performed autopsies on people who were killed by the blast, they found that most victims had died from breathing in the ash. It filled their lungs and windpipes.

Some dead bodies had so much ash in them that it dulled the blades of the doctors' scalpels!

It took more than ten weeks to clean up all the ash in Washington. When it was almost gone, people began to relax. Maybe now their lives could get back to normal.

But then, on July 22, the mountain erupted again. More smoke and ash came billowing out.

This time it drifted west and landed on Portland and Seattle.

People began to wonder—would it ever stop?

For the next several months, the mountain kept rumbling. Bursts of steam here. Gas and hot rocks there.

Then it was quiet for a while.

Years went by, and every so often the volcano spit hot ash into the air.

But at the same time, signs of life began to return to the mountain.

Even that first summer, a few flowers pushed up through the thick layers of ash to bloom on the barren, rocky volcano top.

And to everyone's surprise, a few animal species reappeared. Some of them had survived the blast!

Tiny pocket gophers, who lived in burrows underground, had been protected from the eruption. So were some mice, weasels, and ants.

Slowly but surely, other animals began to wander back into the blast zone. And wind blew seeds that landed on the now-fertile soil. Some of them sprouted and bloomed.

The more the plants grew, the more the animals returned. Little by little, the chain of life was renewed.

In 1982, the blast zone was declared a national monument. Four years later, a visitors' center opened on the mountain, featuring films, photographs, and other information about the blast. Roads and trails were cut so that people could climb the volcano and peer right into the smoking crater itself.

And much of the destruction was left just as it happened. Many cars and trucks that had been trapped in the blast were left for people to see.

Lu and Mike Moore's car is one of them. It is part of the Mount St. Helens National Volcanic Monument now.

For several years the mountain continued to erupt with small bursts of hot ash and steam.

But it wasn't exploding like a bomb anymore. In time, the people who lived nearby got used to it.

Even the survivors got used to it.

"I don't think about it much," says Terra Moore, the youngest survivor.

She was the baby in the backpack—only three months old when the mountain blew. She is a teenager now.

"I'm sure the mountain will erupt again," she says. "But I don't worry about it at all."

Other teenagers feel the same way. They were too young to remember the blast. Some of them would even like to see the mountain explode again.

But will that happen in their lifetime? Probably not.

Right now the mountain is trying to rebuild

itself. Magma from inside the earth has already pushed up into a huge crater at the top, forming what scientists call a lava dome. Each year the dome grows a little bigger.

Most likely, Mount St. Helens will quietly continue to build a lava dome and remain dormant for another one hundred years.

But what about all the *other* volcanoes in the Cascade Range?

Right next to St. Helens stand the two angry warriors of the Native American tales, Mount Adams and Mount Hood.

Will they wage their fiery battle again, exploding with smoke and brimstone on the people who live nearby?

And what about Mount Rainier? Mount Baker? Lassen Peak?

Scientists think that Mount Baker is the one most likely to erupt. In 1975, it sprang to life for a short time, sending up sprays of smoke.

But no one can say exactly when the next link in the Ring of Fire will send out a fiery message of doom. The science of predicting volcanic eruptions is still very young.

Scientists only know that eventually at least 6 of the 17 Cascade mountains are likely to erupt again.

But when…?

Mount St. Helens Facts

Most of the numbers in this book, including the ones below, are estimates.

Power of the eruption

Height of mountain before the blast.....9,677 feet

Height of mountain after the blast........8,363 feet

Amount of ash hurled
into the air ....400 million tons

Force of eruption ....10 to 50 megaton bombs

Temperature of gas and
ash in the blast..............................900° Fahrenheit

Distance the blast was heard ....690 miles

Volume of water
in the mudflow............................46 billion gallons

How far the blast zone reached...............17 miles

Length of eruption ....9 hours

Maximum height of ash cloud.................16 miles

Top speed of mudflow ....50 mph

Number of days it took for
ash cloud to circle the earth 17

Width of the crater
remaining after the blast..............................1 mile

Depth of the crater ....1 mile

The victims

Number of people who died 61

Number of bodies never found.........................27

Large mammals killed....................................8,400

Small mammals killed 40,000

Fish killed..11,000,000

Motorists stranded because of ash...............3,000

Property damage

Bridges damaged or destroyed by mudflow 8

Homes damaged or destroyed 300

Board feet of lumber destroyed............4.7 billion

Area of forest flattened ....230 square miles

Number of lakes destroyed by mudflow...........26

Total estimated dollar value
of property damage.................................$1 billion

Want to Know More?

Museum

Mount St. Helens National Volcanic Monument
Visitors' Center
3029 Spirit Lake Highway
Castle Rock, Wash. 98611
(206) 274-2103

Books

Volcano and Earthquake by Susanna Van Rose
(Eyewitness Books, Alfred A. Knopf, 1992, 64
pages). Beautiful color photographs and illustrations on every page help explain how volcanoes
work. It includes details about the biggest erup-

tions in history, how to survive disasters, volcanoes on other planets, and more.

How Did We Find Out About Volcanoes? by Isaac Asimov (Walker and Company, 1981, 64 pages). This is a historical look at some of the most active volcanoes of all time, including Mount Vesuvius and Mount Pelée.

Volcano: The Eruption and Healing of Mount St. Helens by Patricia Lauber (Bradbury Press, 1986, 60 pages). With detailed scientific information about the eruption and the aftermath, this book will show you how life forms returned to Mount St. Helens after the blast.

When you are older, you might want to read *Fire Mountain: The Eruptions of Mount St. Helens* by William Boly (Cathco Publishing, Inc., 1980, 74 pages). It is full of color photographs of the mountain, and is available at the Mount St. Helens Visitors' Center.

Mount St. Helens: A Sleeping Volcano Awakes by Marian T. Place (Dodd, Mead, 1981, 158 pages). A fascinating look at the entire event, this book includes survivors' stories and eyewitness accounts.

Index